BABY LLAMAS

by Martha London

Cody Koala

An Imprint of Pop!
popbooksonline.com

abdobooks.com
Published by Pop!, a division of ABDO, PO Box 398166, Minneapolis, Minnesota 55439. Copyright © 2021 by POP, LLC. International copyrights reserved in all countries. No part of this book may be reproduced in any form without written permission from the publisher. Pop!™ is a trademark and logo of POP, LLC.

Printed in the United States of America, North Mankato, Minnesota

052020
092020

THIS BOOK CONTAINS RECYCLED MATERIALS

Cover Photo: Shutterstock Images
Interior Photos: Shutterstock Images, 1, 5 (top), 5 (bottom right), 6, 9, 15 (top), 20–21; Dr. Enrique Chavez/Alamy, 5 (bottom left); blickwinkel/Alamy, 10; Oliver Dixon/Alamy, 13; Florian Kopp/imageBROKER/Alamy, 15 (bottom left); Jiri Vondrous/Alamy, 15 (bottom right); GM Photo Images/Alamy, 17; Danita Delimont/Alamy, 19

Editor: Nick Rebman
Series Designer: Christine Ha

Library of Congress Control Number: 2019955134
Publisher's Cataloging-in-Publication Data
Names: London, Martha, author.
Title: Baby llamas / by Martha London
Description: Minneapolis, Minnesota : POP!, 2021 | Series: Baby farm animals | Includes online resources and index
Identifiers: ISBN 9781532167461 (lib. bdg.) | ISBN 9781532168567 (ebook)
Subjects: LCSH: Llamas--Juvenile literature. | Baby farm animals--Juvenile literature. | Animal babies--Juvenile literature.
Classification: DDC 636.2/966--dc23

Hello! My name is

Cody Koala

Pop open this book and you'll find QR codes like this one, loaded with information, so you can learn even more!

Scan this code* and others like it while you read, or visit the website below to make this book pop.

popbooksonline.com/baby-llamas

*Scanning QR codes requires a web-enabled smart device with a QR code reader app and a camera.

Table of Contents

Chapter 1
Fluffy Fur. 4

Chapter 2
From Milk to Grass. 8

Chapter 3
Growing Up 14

Chapter 4
A Llama with a Job 18

Making Connections 22
Glossary. 23
Index 24
Online Resources 24

Fluffy Fur

Baby llamas are called crias. Crias are **mammals**. They are born with soft fur. Most female llamas have one baby at a time.

Watch a video here!

Baby llamas are born during the day. They stand and walk within one hour of birth. Baby llamas stay close to their mothers. Mother llamas protect their babies.

Llamas are related to camels.

From Milk to Grass

Baby llamas get most of their **nutrients** from their mothers' milk. Crias drink milk for six months. Then they eat solid food.

9

Llamas have split upper lips. They do not have upper teeth. They have teeth only on the bottom. Llamas use their lips and teeth to pull grass out of the ground.

Llamas sometimes spit to keep predators away.

Llamas have two large toes on each foot. Each toe has a nail and a padded heel. Llamas' feet are good at gripping the ground. They can walk on rocky surfaces without falling.

ear
eye
neck
leg
toes

Chapter 3

Growing Up

Llamas are **social**. They live in groups called **herds**. Llamas spend their days **grazing** in fields. They get most of their water from the food they eat.

Learn more here!

Female llamas grow up quickly. They become adults after one year. Male llamas grow up more slowly. They become adults after three years. An adult llama can grow to be 6 feet (1.8 m) tall.

Chapter 4

A Llama with a Job

Farmers keep llamas for a few different reasons. One reason is that llamas have a soft **undercoat**. Farmers cut this soft fur. They use it to create yarn.

Learn more here!

Some llamas are guard animals. Farmers use these llamas to protect sheep. Other llamas are

pack animals. They carry
loads. Llamas can carry up
to 75 pounds (34 kg) over
long distances.

Making Connections

Text-to-Self

Would you want to pet a llama? Describe what its fur might feel like.

Text-to-Text

Have you read books about other mammals? How are those mammals similar to and different from llamas?

Text-to-World

Why might llamas make good pack animals?

Glossary

graze – to eat grass or other plants in a field.

herd – a large group of animals that live and travel together.

mammal – a type of animal that has hair or fur and feeds milk to its young.

nutrient – part of food that humans, animals, and plants need to stay strong and healthy.

social – enjoying the company of others.

undercoat – the soft layer of fur under the rough outer hair.

Index

feet, 12

fur, 4, 18

grazing, 14

herds, 14

milk, 8

pack animals, 21

teeth, 11

Online Resources

popbooksonline.com

Thanks for reading this Cody Koala book!

Scan this code* and others like it in this book, or visit the website below to make this book pop!

popbooksonline.com/baby-llamas

*Scanning QR codes requires a web-enabled smart device with a QR code reader app and a camera.